AF572304

By

Bruce Weber

Edited By

Michael E. Goodman

CRESTWOOD HOUSE

Mankato, Minnesota
U.S.A.

Weber, Bruce.
Sparky Anderson.

(SCU-2)
SUMMARY: Discusses Sparky Anderson's early career as a baseball player in minor and major leagues and his later success as manager of the Detroit Tigers.
1. Anderson, Sparky, 1934- —Juvenile literature. 2. Baseball—United States—Managers—Biography—Juvenile literature. [1. Anderson, Sparky, 1934- . 2. Baseball—Managers. 3. Baseball players.] I. Goodman, Michael E. II. Title. III. Series.
GV865.A48W43 1988 796.357'092'4—dc19 [B] [92] 88-14985
ISBN 0-89686-379-4

International Standard Book Number:
0-89686-379-4

Library of Congress Catalog Card Number:
88-14985

PHOTO CREDITS

Cover: Focus West (Ron Vesely)
Sports Illustrated: (Heinz Kluetmeier) 7, 11, 20-21, 36, 38-39, 40, 46
Focus West: (Ron Vesely) 8, 12, 27, 44-45; (J. Rettaliata) 4;
(Fred Vuich) 16, 28; (John Biever) 19, 24; (Dave Stock) 23, 31; (Rick Stewart) 33, 43
Wide World Photos: 15

Produced by Carnival Enterprises.

TABLE OF CONTENTS

DETROIT
Rawlings

WE'LL BE BACK

The pacing was over. So was the season. The short gray-haired man wearing the Detroit Tigers uniform would do no more yelling this year. His team had played 167 games since opening day, including five games in the 1987 American League Championship Series. There'd be no more games until 1988.

George (Sparky) Anderson sat with his players on the bench at Tiger Stadium. They stared out at the ballfield. The Minnesota Twins were the new American League champs. They were hugging each other. They were falling onto the ground with teammates, pounding them with joy. But, aside from the celebrating Twins, the stadium was quiet. Most of the disappointed Tiger fans were heading for the exits. Sparky and his players were disappointed, too. They felt that they should have been doing the celebrating. Slowly the Tigers—and their manager—realized that it was all over.

Sparky bent down and picked up a Tiger cap. One of the players must have dropped it, he thought. He looked at the old-fashioned "D" on the front. We'll be back, Sparky told himself. We've always come back before.

Slowly he walked down the runway and turned into the hushed locker room. He moved past his players' lockers and looked at the names written above them—Alan Trammell, Lou Whitaker, Kirk Gibson, Jack Morris. Yes, Sparky thought, we'll be back. There's plenty of talent on this team.

After the scheduled meeting with the press and a visit to the Twins' dressing room, Sparky began pulling off his Tiger

Sparky Anderson plans his team's next move.

uniform for the last time in 1987. Already he was thinking about the next season. Who will be our regular right fielder? What will happen with free agents? We've got to be ready, he thought. But we'll be back.

GROWING UP IN SOUTH DAKOTA

About 40 miles down the road from Sioux Falls, South Dakota, is the little town of Bridgewater. Today there is a big billboard at the town line. It tells anyone passing through that this is the home of George (Sparky) Anderson, the famous baseball manager. The ballfield in town is named for Sparky, too. He is Bridgewater's favorite son.

George Lee Anderson was born in Bridgewater on February 22, 1934. In 1934, the United States was in the depths of the Great Depression. George was one of five Anderson children. There wasn't much money, and that made George dream about better times. He promised himself that one day he would have enough clothing to wear a new outfit every day (that's one reason why Sparky is one of baseball's snappiest dressers today).

George's father, uncle, and grandfather were house painters. If it weren't for baseball, Sparky says today, he probably would have become a painter, too. "I still enjoy painting," he says. "When you paint, you have time to dream. There's not much else to think about. You can't get into much

George with his wife Carol.

trouble. If you make a mistake, you can cover it up with paint. I really like that."

Sports were always a part of young George's life. His father played semi-pro baseball. George and his family would pile into the family car to go watch his father play.

There were only 632 people in Bridgewater, but that didn't stop the young people from having a good time. When the pond froze over during the winter, hockey games were organized.

"We didn't have a puck," Anderson remembers. "We used an old can."

Today Sparky looks back at the time in Bridgewater as one of the happiest in his life. He returns to Bridgewater to visit from time to time. He often takes part in fund-raising projects in his old home town. He hasn't forgotten Bridgewater, and Bridgewater hasn't forgotten him either.

THE L.A. TEENAGER

It was tough for George's father, uncle, and grandfather to make a living in South Dakota. They could paint houses only during the summer. There were odd jobs, of course, but they were hard to get. With five children to feed and clothe, George's father had to make a decision. He had been born in South Dakota, but he decided to move his whole family to sunny California.

"Nine people leaving Bridgewater made quite a dent in the city's population," remembers Sparky.

Watching the players closely.

In November 1942, three months before George's ninth birthday, the Andersons arrived in Los Angeles. They moved to 35th Street just off Vermont Avenue. Then, as now, it was one of L.A.'s toughest neighborhoods. It was also just a couple of blocks away from the University of Southern California (USC) campus.

The Andersons were a close-knit family. George's family lived in one house with his grandparents. Next door lived his uncle's family, with four more kids. George's grandmother did all the sewing for the 15 Andersons, and his mother was the family baker. They were poor, but they didn't feel poor. There was plenty of love to go around for all the children.

Every day George would walk past Bovard Field where the USC Trojans played baseball. Finding a ball in the bushes one day, George rushed in and returned it to coach Rod Dedeaux. Dedeaux liked the young man and offered him a job as the Trojans' batboy. A love affair was born between George Anderson and USC. Though Sparky claims he was never smart enough to think about going to college, he immediately became Southern Cal's biggest fan. He still is today. In fact, he has been honored as one of the Trojans' top "alumni supporters."

George's work with the USC team helped him develop a total love for baseball. When he went to Dorsey High School in Los Angeles, he naturally turned to baseball as his game. He also began to date Carol Valle. They had met in the fifth grade and have been together ever since.

At Dorsey High, George played shortstop. His grammar school buddy, Billy Consolo, played third. Together they

Sparky's home is filled with photos and other baseball souvenirs.

helped the team win 42 straight games. In southern California, where the nation's best high school baseball was played, Dorsey was the best. Team scouts from many major league teams paid close attention to Dorsey's players, including the shortstop.

At graduation time, the Brooklyn Dodgers sent scout Lefty Phillips to sign up George. The Dodgers offered George a contract to play for their Santa Barbara farm team in the California State League. That was near the bottom of organized baseball. George's contract paid $3,000 per year—and that included his bonus!

Meanwhile, the Boston Red Sox took a fancy to George's pal Billy and gave him a $65,000 bonus. That was a lot of money.

"It figured," says Sparky today. "Billy could flat out play. Me? I was very mediocre, very average. But the money was about right." And so George Lee Anderson set out to make his fortune in the game he loved—baseball.

THE LONG ROAD

When George signed with the Dodgers' team in Santa Barbara, there was no glamour. Santa Barbara was a Class C team. They don't have Class C teams today, but back in 1953, Class C meant a very unimportant team in the minor leagues.

That didn't matter to George. It was a chance to get paid to play the game he loved. He again played shortstop and didn't do too badly. He played in 141 games and hit .263. He hit five homers. That didn't seem like much at the time, but he would only hit 19 home runs in his entire pro career.

At the end of the season, George's friend, scout Lefty Phillips, came to visit. "It's going to be tough for you," said Lefty. "Everything you do will come hard." Lefty was telling

In 1953 Sparky began his baseball career as a minor league player.

the truth. For all of his love of baseball, George wasn't a gifted player. He didn't have the kind of skills that made superstars. In fact, his throwing arm was so weak that the Dodgers decided to move him to second base.

He spent the 1954 season at Pueblo, Colorado. He had a pretty good year, hitting .296 in 147 games. He also knocked in 62 runs. He was ready to move up again to the next level.

The new team still wasn't the majors, but conditions improved somewhat in the higher minors. The bus rides weren't as long and the lights in the ballparks were better. Better yet, each step up brought the players closer to their goal—the major leagues.

In 1955, while the big-league Brooklyn Dodgers were winning their only world championship, George worked hard playing in the Texas League. George had another solid season and was moved to the Dodgers' top farm team in Montreal. It would be another 13 years before the major leagues would come to Montreal. But the Royals were among the top minor-league outfits.

By now, George Anderson was known as Sparky. A radio announcer had given him the nickname because whenever he was out on the field, his energy seemed to make sparks fly—there was always action around him.

Sparky took another giant stride toward the big leagues by having his best season at bat. During his time in Montreal, he proved to be one of the top double-play makers in the game. He went home in 1957 and played for his old boyhood heroes, the Los Angeles Angels of the Pacific Coast League. Sparky

When the score gets close, a manager needs something to ease the tension.

responded with his best fielding season though his batting average slipped to .260. It was back to Montreal for the 1958 season, Sparky's sixth year in the minors. He was ready for a shot at the majors.

Through Toronto Manager Chuck Dressen, Sparky learned the ins and outs of managing a team.

A MOMENT IN THE MAJORS

What was the best Christmas present Sparky Anderson ever received? Easy. Two days before Christmas in 1958, two months before his 25th birthday, Sparky got an important phone call from the Philadelphia Phillies. They had traded three players to the Los Angeles Dodgers, and Sparky was now the property of the Phillies. He was to report to their spring training camp in February. He was going to the big leagues.

During spring training, the Phillies announced that Sparky Anderson would be their second baseman. He played in 152 of the 154 games and did a fine job on defense. Unfortunately, Sparky who had been an average minor league hitter, became a poor-hitting major leaguer. He came to the plate 477 times and had only 104 hits. That added up to a .218 batting average. He knocked in 34 runs and had nine doubles and three triples, but no home runs.

At the end of the season, the Phillies shipped Sparky back to Toronto and the International League.He would never play in another major League game.

THE MAKING OF A MANAGER

Sparky was disappointed. His chance to be a big leaguer was over. Looking back today, he says, "I was a mediocre ballplayer." But as the 1960 season was set to open, Sparky was upset.

His stay at Toronto, however, turned out to be a blessing. The Toronto manager was Chuck Dressen, a veteran manager in the major and minor leagues.

Chuck Dressen always called Sparky "Little Man." "Little Man," said Chuck Dressen, "you are going to be a fine manager some day. You never miss a sign."

Sparky had loved his one year in the majors, but realized he would never get back there as a player. He began to think about managing.

"Chuck Dressen was the greatest influence on my career as a manager," Sparky still says today. "Dressen was a master at running a pitching staff. He knew when to let a pitcher stay in and when to take him out." These days, it's Sparky Anderson who is the master. He earned his second nickname, "Captain Hook," because he is never shy about giving a pitcher "the hook," and bringing in a new pitcher.

Dressen also taught Sparky how to force the opposing manager to use up his available players during a game. Sparky always thinks two or three moves ahead—that's the Dressen influence.

After an 11-year pro career, 10 of them in the minors, it was clear that George Lee Anderson's future in baseball would not be at second base. When he was asked to take over the Toronto club as the manager in 1964, Sparky was ready. At age 30, with a headful of white hair that made him look 50, Sparky added a new title: Manager.

When he began his managing career, Sparky picked up another nickname—Captain Hook.

After 11 years as a baseball player, Sparky was ready to take on a manager's position.

THE LONG ROAD BACK

The hardest thing for a manager to do is manage his friends. But that's what first-time manager Sparky Anderson had to do. He moved directly from second base to the dugout. It wasn't the easiest way to break in to managing. Still, Sparky did a fair job. Toronto had a winning record in 1964, but finished fifth in the league.

Sparky expected to be back in 1965. It didn't happen. The Boston Red Sox took over the Toronto team and put in their own manager. Sparky didn't know what would happen next. He quickly found out.

Bob Howsam of the St. Louis Cardinals called and asked, "How would you like to manage our Rock Hill team in the Western Carolinas League?"

Sparky accepted, then grabbed a map—he had no idea where Rock Hill was. He did know, however, that he was moving from the top of the minor leagues to the bottom. He would be traveling in buses again.

When Sparky arrived in South Carolina, he brought 11 years of experience as a player and one as a manager. He also brought one of the hottest tempers in baseball. Once again, he was making sparks fly. But these weren't the sparks of energy and enthusiasm he'd shown at second base. These were sparks of anger and frustration. He screamed at his players. He bumped umpires. He was booted out of games. But his temper didn't work with these young people; most of them were awful players.

When Sparky thinks an umpire has made the wrong call, he's quick to add his opinion.

KING
25

The Western Carolinas League split the season into two parts. Rock Hill finished eighth—and last—in the first half. Sparky quickly decided that something had to change. In the second half, he controlled himself and became a teacher. He learned to be patient. Rock Hill finished first in the second half. Then they won the playoffs to take the 1965 league title. That, Sparky said to himself, is more like it!

He moved up the managers' ladder. In 1966 he made the playoffs but lost with St. Petersburg of the Florida State League; in 1967, he made the playoffs with Modesto of the California League, but lost again; in 1968, he made the playoffs with Ashville (North Carolina) of the Southern League and this time, he won the pennant.

Big-league people took notice. Everywhere Sparky went, the team got better. Not many managers could say that.

When the San Diego Padres joined the National League in 1969, they looked to this old-looking young man. Sparky became the third base coach in the Padres' first season. He loved being back in the majors. He thought San Diego would be a good spot to move into a manager's office, but he had learned to be patient. He was prepared to wait.

In October 1969, Sparky's old friend, Lefty Phillips, called him. Lefty was the Dodger scout who had first signed young George Anderson to a pro contract. Now Lefty was manager of the California Angels. Lefty wanted Sparky on his 1970 coaching staff. Sparky said yes. He would be happy to coach in Anaheim.

The following day, Sparky's phone rang again. It was Bob

Patience and careful instruction have helped Sparky's teams win games.

Howsam. He had given Sparky the manager's job in Rock Hill. Now Bob was general manager of the Cincinnati Reds. "How would you like to be the new Cincinnati manager?" said Howsam. Sparky jumped at the chance. He turned down the coaching job with the Angels. He knew Lefty would understand. He quickly accepted the job as the Reds' field general. At age 35, he was the game's youngest manager.

THE BIG RED MACHINE

Sparky was in an unusual and tough spot. Most new big-league managers have spent long careers as big-league players. Some spend many years as minor-league managers—at top levels. Almost all take over clubs that have had poor records. They often have little talent to play with. None of the above was true for Sparky Anderson.

Sparky had played only one year of big-league ball. Sparky had managed only four years in the minors—only one at the top (AAA) level. In addition, the Reds had plenty of talent. The players just didn't always play well or try hard enough. Sparky had to change things quickly. He had a contract for only one year. He had to prove himself right away.

The Cincinnati newspapers didn't exactly welcome Sparky's arrival. "Sparky Who?" read the headlines. "Nobody knew me from nothing," said Sparky. "Bob Howsam really took a chance with me."

Sparky took over a team with great untapped talent. Pete Rose, the second baseman, would become baseball's all-time

Getting ready for another win.

leading hit man. The shortstop was Dave Concepcion, who would become an all-star. Other stars were Tony Perez, Bobby Tolan, Lee May, and Hal McRae. Sparky's team had speed, defense, and offense—just about everything a winner needed. And for the team's foundation, Sparky had baseball's top catcher, Johnny Bench. The "Big Red Machine" was about to be born.

"I know I had to shake things up," said Sparky. He gave his coaches a lot of control. He appointed fiery Pete Rose as team captain. He met with team leaders often and asked for their advice and help. He gambled on the field and didn't always "follow the book." He changed pitchers frequently. He and the Reds were exciting.

They were also winners. In Sparky's first year, the ballclub won 70 of their first 100 games and finished the season with a 102-60 record. They won the National League (NL) West Division by 14½ games. Then they swept the Pirates in three straight games to capture the National League pennant. It was only the second league title in 40 years for the Reds. Although they came up short in the World Series, losing in five games to a great Baltimore Oriole team, it had been a year to remember.

The following year, 1971, was a year to forget. Bothered by injuries, the Reds slumped to a record of 79-83 and finished fourth in the West. It was only a brief pause for the Machine.

In 1972, another future superstar, Joe Morgan, joined the team. He made a good team even better. The Reds

"Let's get this game going!"

immediately returned to the top of the NL West. That year they captured their second NL title in three years.

The World Series is often called the "Fall Classic." It was truly a classic in 1972. The Reds lost in seven games to the powerful Oakland A's. Six of the seven games were decided by one run. This World Series was not for people with weak hearts. The Oakland manager was Dick Williams. "Dick outmanaged me," said Sparky. "We should have won. When a team wins four one-run games, they are well-managed. These were two outstanding teams. Dick Williams made the difference."

1975 & 1976: WINNING SEASONS

By 1975, the Big Red Machine was ready to run at top speed. That's the year Cincinnati went 108-54 to capture the NL West again. The Reds swept the Pirates in the playoffs and faced the Boston Red Sox, the American League champs, in the World Series.

The Red Sox were very tough. They had great hitters and great pitchers. But the Cincinnati Reds were just an eyelash better. After five games, Cincy led three games to two.

The teams came to Boston—and so did the rain. For four days, the teams watched it pour. Finally game six got underway. The Reds led 6-3 in the eighth. But a three-run pinch hit homer by the Red Sox tied it. Finally, in the twelfth inning, Boston's Carlton Fisk homered to win the game, 7-6.

An autographed ball from Sparky Anderson is a real collector's item!

The Series went to a seventh game.

In that final game, Boston jumped into the lead, 3-0, in the third, but the Reds battled back. They won the game with relief pitcher Clay Carroll in the top of the ninth. The Reds were world champions! It had been a typical Sparky Anderson series. Captain Hook had used nine different pitchers in the series. Eight different pitchers worked in the sixth game alone.

Cincinnati won only 102 games in 1976, six fewer than the year before. But they dashed past the Phillies in three straight games in the playoffs. Only the New York Yankees stood between Sparky's gang and another world championship.

Sparky was ready. Johnny Bench was his catcher, Dave Concepcion played shortstop, and Pete Rose was at third. The Reds swept the series, four games to none. This was the Big Red Machine at its best. Seven Reds starters hit over .300. It was an awesome display. Sparky and the Machine owned the world.

FIRED

The winning seasons didn't last much longer. In 1977, the Reds slipped to second in the West. In 1978, the team was second again after a 92-69 season. Not bad by most standards, but a disappointment in Cincinnati. After all, the Reds had finished in first place for five of the previous seven seasons.

Still, when Sparky went to a Los Angeles hotel in late 1978, he was feeling pretty good; the Reds had just returned from

In 1979 after he'd been fired from the Cincinnati Reds, Sparky knew he'd be hired by another ball club soon.

an exhibition series in Japan where they received a warm welcome from the Japanese fans. The new Cincinnati president, Dick Wagner, wanted to meet with him. "He probably wants to talk about players," Sparky figured. "He wants my opinion." Wrong! Dick Wagner had decided to fire Sparky.

Sparky left the meeting in shock. But not for long. As always, Sparky made up his mind to turn a loss into a win. "You can't keep Sparky Anderson down," he thought.

TURNING A LOSS INTO A WIN

Baseball people knew it would not be long before Sparky would be back. He was in no rush, however. He still had a year left on his contract with the Reds and would be paid even if he didn't work. But he didn't want to sit around and do nothing.

So Sparky the manager became Sparky the broadcaster. He began announcing games on radio and TV. He was the "color man," the expert who explains what is going on. His grammar wasn't very good, but he was able to explain the finer points of the game to listeners and viewers. He was an instant success as an announcer.

"It was a lot of fun," Sparky remembers. "It doesn't take much to be a good color man. You just talk about a game you're suppose to know. You don't have to be a genius."

Sparky was good at radio and TV work, but he was a better manager than talker. He figured someone would need him as a manager pretty soon.

It didn't take long. One-third of the way through the 1979 season, the call came. Les Moss wasn't getting the job done at Detroit. After a couple of meetings between Sparky and Detroit officials, a decision was made. Les Moss was out; Sparky Anderson was in. Armed with a five-year contract, Sparky was back where he belonged — in the manager's office.

NEW MAN IN THE MOTOR CITY

When new manager Sparky Anderson met with the Detroit press, he said, "I have a five-year contract. We will win a pennant before it runs out."

Was Sparky crazy to make that kind of promise? Most people thought so. "Anderson Announces Five-Year Plan," read the headlines. Talk about making pressure for yourself!

Even Sparky thought he might have gone too far. At that time, the Detroit Tigers didn't have the talent that his old Cincinnati team had. Though the Tigers went 56-50 for the rest of 1979, they still finished fifth in the American League East. There was a long road ahead. "I knew the people wanted me to give them hope," Sparky recalls. "So I gave them hope. But deep down, I didn't believe it would happen."

Sparky has his own special style. He tries to make his players feel good about themselves. This was especially important with a young team like the Tigers. Slowly Sparky began to build his ballclub.

The 1980 Tigers remained in fifth place. The team was gaining respect, however. In 1981, Detroit was still in fourth place when the ballplayers went on strike and missed 53 games. When the strike was over, baseball Commissioner Bowie Kuhn announced that the season would be split. The first half was over; the teams would start again at 0-0.

"Just like in the minors," thought Sparky Anderson. He

remembered his Western Carolinas League days. His teams always played much better in the second half. It was true again. Detroit went 29-23 and finished the season in second place.

The Tigers slipped to fourth place again in '82, but they really put it together in 1983. Sparky was in the fourth year of his five-year plan. The Tigers went 92-70, good for a second place finish in the AL East. They were on their way.

Pressure really built for 1984. This was Sparky's fifth year in the Motor City. His contract had already been extended to 1986. But Tiger fans didn't forget Sparky's promises made in 1979. The fifth year was here.

THE FIFTH YEAR BEGINS

Before the 1984 season, Sparky studied his team. He had fine pitching, a great outfield, and a super double-play combo, Lou Whitaker and Alan Trammell. "Looking good," said Sparky, as spring training ended.

Even he didn't know how good. The Tigers won their first nine games. By May the Tigers had won 35 of their first 40 games. It was the fastest start in major league history.

Always thinking ahead, Sparky gave his substitute players plenty of playing time during the streak. He had catchers playing in the infield. He had back-ups in the outfield. He gave his regulars lots of rest. "They'll be fresher during the pennant run," said Sparky.

"We'd better win this," Sparky told his players that summer. "If we don't, the fans will lynch us."

Armed with a fat lead, Detroit played like champs all year, never losing more than four games in a row. When it was all over, they finished 104-58, 15 games ahead of second-place Toronto.

Sparky felt great. He became the first manager to win 100 or more games in each league. Still, Sparky knew that a division title wouldn't be enough. If the Tigers didn't win the AL championship and the World Series, people would forget the great season.

When he was hired by the Detroit Tigers, Sparky promised a pennant within five years.

THE CHAMPS

With the American League championship on the line, Anderson turned to an old friend, pitcher Milt Wilcox. Detroit had won the first two games of the playoffs against Kansas City. One more win would do it. Sparky gave the ball to Milt. "Win it for me," the white-haired manager said.

Reporters are always curious about Sparky's future plans.

Wilcox took to the mound and pitched like he never had before. When it was over, the Tigers had won the American League championship.

Wilcox was just one of many heroes. But the day was special for him. "I didn't understand Sparky at first," he said. "I wasn't always sure what he was talking about. But I've

learned. He handles his players well. He makes everyone feel a part of the team."

Now the San Diego Padres stood between the Tigers and a world championship. San Diego was led by manager Dick Williams. How many times had Sparky's path crossed Williams'? Beating Williams would cap a dream season.

The 1984 World Series started well with Detroit winning Game 1. Then San Diego snatched Game 2. The pressure on Sparky was mounting, but the Tigers held on to win Games 3 and 4. The series ended the next day with an 8-4 Tiger victory!

It was a sweet victory for Sparky Anderson. Detroit's first World Series title in 16 years was his first title in eight years. He had made good on his five-year plan. He also became the first manager to win World Series titles in both leagues. Quite a record!

THE COMEBACK OF 1987

Following the super 1984 season, everyone figured the Tigers were a cinch to repeat in 1985. They were disappointed, though.

Detroit slumped to third place in the AL East with a record of 84-77. They finished third again in 1986. The record improved a little to 87-75. But the Tigers had become "just another team."

Going into 1987, most experts picked the Tigers third or fourth or even fifth. The Boston Red Sox were super in 1986.

Sparky escapes from the baseball field to the golf course.

The Toronto Blue Jays were loaded. And the Yankees had really improved. But Sparky was quietly confident. He knew he had good talent on his team. Gibson had plenty of power in right. Morris led a pitching staff that included Walt Terrell and Frank Tanana. He knew, however, that his young players would have to come through. They did.

Rookie Mike Henneman came out of the bullpen to go 11-2 with seven saves. Rookie Matt Nokes hit 32 homers and had 87 RBIs. Rookie Jeff Robinson won nine games. Veterans helped, too. First baseman Darrell Evans hit 34 homers and knocked in 99 runs. Larry Herndon hit .373 against left-handers.

Still, with eight games left in the season, Detroit trailed first-place Toronto by 3½ games. Hopeless? Almost, but not quite.

On a Sunday afternoon in Toronto, the Jays were just about to wrap up the pennant with a win. But Kirk Gibson tied the game 1-1 in the ninth. In the 13th, the Tigers won the game with a bloop single. Now the gap was 2½ games.

When Toronto arrived in Detroit the following Friday, the gap was down to one game. Sparky sent Doyle Alexander to the mound. The Tigers won 3-2 and the pennant race was tied. Detroit won the next game 3-2 to lead Toronto by one game.

On Sunday, Detroit wrapped it up. Herndon homers. Detroit leads 1-0. Tigers win the title with a 98-64 record. That was an 11-game improvement over 1986.

In a tough pennant race, Sparky began to feel as old as he looked. His hair couldn't get any whiter, and the lines in his

The 1987 pennant race was a tough one for Sparky and his team.

Detroit Tiger Matt Nokes receives some pointers from his manager.

NIKE

face seemed to get deeper.

The Minnesota Twins ended the Tigertown joy in the 1987 playoffs. But Sparky, as always, was proud of his players. He could not wait for 1988.

GEORGE AND SPARKY

"I think I can manage for another ten years," said Sparky at the end of the 1987 season. If he does it, he'll rank among the top managers of all time. With 1,611 wins through 1987, Sparky became No. 11 on the list. At that rate, ten more years would bring him to 2,506 wins. Only Connie Mack and John McGraw have won more.

Whether he stays for another decade or not, Sparky has made his mark. The one-time young hothead has become one of the game's coolest managers. A great teacher, Sparky is outstanding with young players.

Meanwhile, he remains loyal to his roots. He still lives close to his mother. He is still married to his fifth-grade sweetheart. He still has his high school teammate, Billy Consolo, at his side in the Tiger dugout.

At the start, there were two very different people. George Anderson was the loyal son, loyal husband, loyal friend. Sparky Anderson was the fiery man in the dugout and on the field. If Sparky acted up, George would apologize.

Today, as he has matured, Sparky and George have become one man. What they have become is one of the greatest managers in baseball history.

Sparky is ready to manage baseball teams for another ten years.

SPARKY ANDERSON'S PROFESSIONAL STATISTICS

RECORD AS A PLAYER

Year	Club
1953	Santa Barbara
1954	Pueblo
1955	Fort Worth
1956	Montreal
1957	Los Angeles
1958	Montreal
1959	Philadelphia (majors)
1960-1963	Toronto

RECORD AS A MANAGER

Year	Club
1964	Toronto
1965	Rock Hill
1966	St. Petersburg
1967	Modesto
1968	Ashville
1970-1978	Cincinnati (majors)
1979-1987	Detroit (majors)

CHAMPIONSHIP SERIES WINS

Year	Club
1970	Cincinnati
1972-1973	Cincinnati
1975-1976	Cincinnati
1984	Detroit
1987	Detroit

WORLD SERIES WINS

Year	Club
1970	Cincinnati
1972	Cincinnati
1975-1976	Cincinnati
1984	Detroit